Baboons

ABDO
Publishing Company

A Buddy Book
by
Julie Murray

VISIT US AT
www.abdopub.com

Published by Buddy Books, an imprint of ABDO Publishing Company, 4940 Viking Drive, Suite 622, Edina, Minnesota 55435. Copyright © 2002 by Abdo Consulting Group, Inc. International copyrights reserved in all countries. No part of this book may be reproduced in any form without written permission from the publisher.

Printed in the United States.

Edited by: Christy DeVillier
Contributing Editors: Matt Ray, Michael P. Goecke
Graphic Design: Maria Hosley
Image Research: Deborah Coldiron
Photographs: Eyewire

Library of Congress Cataloging-in-Publication Data

Murray, Julie, 1969-
  Baboons/Julie Murray.
      p. cm. — (Animal kingdom)
  Summary: An introduction to the physical characteristics, habitats, behavior, and different types of baboons, large monkeys who live in troops in Africa and the Middle East.
  ISBN 1-57765-711-X
    1. Baboons—Juvenile literature. [1. Baboons.] I. Title. II. Animal kingdom
  (Edina, Minn.)

QL737.P93 M87 2002
599.8'65—dc21

                                                    2001053382

Contents

Old World Monkeys

Baboons, guenons, and macaques are all Old World monkeys. Old World monkeys live in Asia and Africa. Long ago, people called Africa and Asia the "Old World." This is where Old World monkeys get their name.

Baboons have thumbs.

Old World monkeys are primates. People and apes are primates, too. Primates have large brains. Most primates have five fingers on each hand. One of these fingers is a thumb. A thumb allows people and other primates to hold and grab things.

Baboons

There are different kinds of baboons. There are yellow baboons, chacma baboons, hamadryas baboons, gelada baboons, and guinea baboons. The best-known baboon is the olive baboon. The olive baboon's name comes from its olive-brown coat.

An olive baboon.

What They Look Like

Baboons are big monkeys. Some male baboons can weigh over 100 pounds (45 kg). Female baboons are much smaller than males.

Baboons have rough hair covering most of their bodies. These primates have large heads and long, sharp teeth. A baboon's muzzle is like a dog's muzzle.

Adult baboons are much bigger than baby baboons.

Where They Live

Baboons live mainly in Africa. Some live in Saudi Arabia and other parts of the Middle East. Forests, mountains, and savannas are places where baboons can live.

Baboons live mostly on the ground. They often sleep in trees or on cliffs. This helps to keep them safe from predators.

Some baboons live on cliffs.

Social Animals

Baboons are social animals. Social animals like baboons communicate with each other. A friendly greeting is touching noses for some baboons. Barking, yawning, and staring are other ways baboons communicate.

Grooming is another way for baboons to be social. Baboons groom each other often. They pick insects, dirt, and twigs off each other. Grooming helps baboons stay friendly with one another.

Baboons often groom one another.

Troops

Social animals like to be around each other. So, baboons live together in groups, or troops. These troops can have between 10 and 200 baboons. Females often outnumber the males in baboon troops.

Living in troops helps to keep baboons safe from predators.

The leaders of baboon troops are male. These leaders decide when to get food. They make sure all the baboons follow troop rules.

Predators

One predator of baboons is the leopard. A leopard will hunt one baboon. But they do not often go after a troop of baboons. This is why baboons often stay near their troop. It is the best way for them to guard against predators.

Baboons must watch out for leopards.

Baboons scare away predators by showing their sharp teeth.

Baboons will do many things to scare away predators. They show their teeth. They stomp their feet. Baboons raise their hair, too.

Eating

Baboons often travel far each day to find food and water. Baboons gather fruit, grass, eggs, roots, and nuts. These monkeys will hunt for food, too. Baboons eat birds, gazelles, and impalas.

Male baboons hunt and eat impalas.

Baby Baboons

Most baby baboons are born six months after the rainy season. A newborn baboon rides on its mother's back. At one month old, a baby baboon can move around on its own.

One-year-old baboons can find their own food. They often stay with their mothers until the age of two. Baboons can live to be 45 years old.

A mother baboon carrying her baby.

Important Words

communicate to give and receive information.

groom to clean and care for.

muzzle the nose and mouth area.

predator an animal that hunts other animals (prey) for food.

primate a group that people, apes, and monkeys belong to.

savanna a grassland with few trees.

social animals that live and communicate with one another.

Web Sites

Baboon Facts

www.mindysmem.org/baboon.html
See pictures and learn more about different
kinds of baboons.

Baboon

www.enchantedlearning.com/subjects/mamm
al/monkey/Baboonprintout.shtml
This web site offers facts and a baboon picture
to print out and color.

African Primates at Home

www.indiana.edu/%7Eprimate/primates.html
See and hear many kinds of African primates at
this site.

Index